FROM THE BELLY:
POETS RESPOND TO GERTRUDE STEIN'S *TENDER BUTTONS*
VOL I

OTHER WORD WORKS ANTHOLOGIES:

Cabin Fever: Poets at Joaquin Miller's Cabin
Jacklyn Potter, Dwaine Reeves, Gary Stein, eds.

Cool Fire
Christopher Bursk, ed.

Whose Woods These Are
Karren L. Alenier, ed.

Winners: A Retrospective of the Washington Prize
Karren L. Alenier, Hilary Tham, Miles David Moore, eds.

Word for Word: 40 Years at The Word Works
Nancy White, ed.

ALSO BY KARREN LALONDE ALENIER:

how we hold on (2021)
The Anima of Paul Bowles (2016)
On a Bed of Gardenias: Jane & Paul Bowles (2012)
The Steiny Road to Operadom: The Making of American Operas (2007)
Gertrude Stein Invents a Jump Early On (2005)
Karren LaLonde Alenier Greatest Hits 1973-2002 (2003)
Looking for Divine Transportation (1999)
Bumper Cars: Gertrude Said She Took Him for a Ride (1996)
The Dancer's Muse (1981)
Wandering on the Outside (1975)

FROM THE BELLY

POETS RESPOND

TO GERTRUDE STEIN'S

TENDER BUTTONS

VOL. I

KARREN L. ALENIER, EDITOR

WITH POEMS BY

Karren L. Alenier, Indran Amirthanayagam, Rae Armantrout,
Mary Armour, Carrie Bennett, Margo Berdeshevsky, Julien Berman,
Andrea Carter Brown, Susana H. Case, Grace Cavalieri, Nikia Chaney,
Roberto Christiano, Henry Crawford, Michael Davis, Denise Duhamel,
Amy Feinstein, Barbara Goldberg, Harold M. Greenwald, Donald Illich,
Jacqueline Johnson, Hiram Larew, JoAnne McFarland, Kevin McLellan,
Nils Michals, Brad Richard, Margery M. Ross, Martha Sanchez-Lowery,
Roger Sedarat, Lisa Sewell, Margo Taft Stever, Miles Waggener,
Lillo Way, Nancy White, Carolyne Wright,
Bill Yarrow, Burgi Zenhaeusern,
& Jason Zuzga

THE WORD WORKS

From the Belly: Poets Respond to Gertrude Stein's Tender Buttons © 2023
Karren LaLonde Alenier

Reproduction of any part of this book
in any form by any means,
electronic or mechanical,
must be with permission
in writing from
the publisher.
Address
inquiries to:
THE WORD WORKS
P.O. Box 42164
Washington, D.C. 20015
editor@wordworksbooks.org

Cover Design: Susan Pearce Design
Cover Art: Grace Cavalieri

Library of Congress Control Number: 2022946619
International Standard Book Number: 978-1-944585-61-7

ACKNOWLEDGMENTS

Special thanks to Lisa Sewell and Bill Yarrow who served as my thought partners in the formulation of this project which ultimately will include three volumes, one for each of the three sections of *Tender Buttons* by Gertrude Stein.

Heart-felt thanks to Nancy White who enthusiastically welcomed the idea for this ambitious project, giving it legs by endorsing its publication, and to my special partner Hal Greenwald who has been a sounding board and coach, anchoring even the dreary details of this enormous project.

Great gratitude to Grace Cavalieri for helping me stand back and envision how this project would work, to Al Filreis for starting me down the *Tender Buttons* yellow brick road, to Barbara Goldberg for always listening to my abstract poems, and to all the poets who accepted their randomly assigned subpoems of *Tender Buttons* and contributed their remarkable poems.

—Karren L. Alenier

The Stein text presented here is as it appears in *Tender Buttons: The Corrected Centennial Edition* edited by Seth Perlow.

The following poems by Karren LaLonde Alenier were previously published in:

Poets Are Present Anthology (DC: Shakespeare Theatre Company, 2015): "Herd Speak"

New Verse News (https://newversenews.blogspot.com/2018/04/state-of-union-dialectic.html): "State of the Union: A Dialectic"

for Ulla Dydo
(1925-2017)

CONTENTS

Introduction ... 9
Invitation ... 11

The Objects of *Tender Buttons* with Responses:

A Carafe, That Is A Blind Glass. ❧ on the matter of being ❧ Karren L. Alenier ... 14
Glazed Glitter. ❧ making Americans ❧ Karren L. Alenier ... 16
A Substance In A Cushion. ❧ the worthy one ❧ Karren L. Alenier ... 18
A Box. ❧ the wars of Leo Stein ❧ Karren L. Alenier ... 20
A Piece Of Coffee. ❧ herd speak: a reflection ❧ Karren L. Alenier ... 22
Dirt And Not Copper. ❧ the entrance: a count off in eights ❧ Karren L. Alenier ... 24
Nothing Elegant. ❧ about the word ❧ Karren L. Alenier ... 26
Mildred's Umbrella. ❧ umbrella suite: a gauge ❧ Karren L. Alenier ... 28
A Method Of A Cloak. ❧ taken for a ride ❧ Karren L. Alenier ... 30
A Red Stamp. ❧ whiff ❧ Karren L. Alenier ... 32
A Box. ❧ a box ❧ Roger Sedarat ... 34
A Plate. ❧ temple and tiger ❧ Michael Davis ... 36
A Seltzer Bottle. ❧ trinken aus "A Seltzer Bottle." ❧ Karren L. Alenier ... 39
A Long Dress. ❧ birth of the long dress made in America ❧ Karren L. Alenier ... 40
A Red Hat. ❧ a red hat ❧ Harold M. Greenwald ... 42
A Blue Coat. ❧ a blue coat ❧ Karren L. Alenier ... 44
A Piano. ❧ an open piano ❧ Henry Crawford ... 46
A Chair. ❧ the entire text is a field ❧ Nils Michals ... 48
A Frightful Release. ❧ the bag dreams ❧ Burgi Zenhaeusern ... 50
A Purse. ❧ two more purses ❧ Denise Duhamel ... 52
A Mounted Umbrella. ❧ returning to the father ❧ Karren L. Alenier ... 54
A Cloth. ❧ rare on rares ❧ Hiram Larew ... 56
More. ❧ less ❧ Indran Amirthanayagam ... 58
A New Cup And Saucer. ❧ entwine ❧ Jacqueline Johnson ... 60
Objects. ❧ To Not OBJECTify ❧ Mary Armour ... 62
Eye Glasses. ❧ a Steinian stethoscope ❧ Karren L. Alenier ... 64
A Cutlet. ❧ portrait of the father ❧ Karren L. Alenier ... 66
Careless Water. ❧ "when you sit down to." ❧ Nikia Chaney ... 68
A Paper. ❧ (rock) paper (scissors) ❧ Andrea Carter Brown ... 70
A Drawing. ❧ the story ands (this is how) ❧ Jason Zuzga ... 72
Water Raining. ❧ water ❧ Nancy White ... 74
Cold Climate. ❧ hat before snow ❧ Grace Cavalieri ... 76

Malachite. ❦ honeycomb ❦ Carrie Bennett . . . 78
An Umbrella. ❦ setting the table ❦ Roberto Christiano . . . 80
A Petticoat. ❦ petticoat ❦ JoAnne McFarland . . . 82
A Waist. ❦ in a change that is remarkable there is no reason to say that there was a time ❦ Miles Waggener . . . 84
A Time To Eat. ❦ gender gluttons ❦ Lillo Way . . . 86
A Little Bit Of A Tumbler. ❦ the rest of time ❦ Lisa Sewell . . . 88
A Fire. ❦ nicely sent(ient) ❦ Bill Yarrow . . . 90
A Handkerchief. ❦ handkerchief ❦ Margery M. Ross . . . 92
Red Roses. ❦ rose recipe ❦ Don Illich . . . 94
In Between. ❦ state of the union: a dialectic with "In Between." ❦ Karren L. Alenier . . . 96
Colored Hats. ❦ colored condoms. ❦ Kevin McLellan . . . 98
A Feather. ❦ the feathered girl ❦ Martha Sanchez-Lowery . . . 100
A Brown. ❦ pandemic buttons ❦ Amy Feinstein . . . 102
A Little Called Pauline. ❦ through a little window to the fairy sea ❦ Karren L. Alenier . . . 104
A Sound. ❦ SOUND of a SONG for the DOO-DA-DAY ❦ Margo Berdeshevsky . . . 106
A Table. ❦ progressively smaller dimensions ❦ Susana H. Case . . . 108
Shoes. ❦ shoe: a Tender Buttons meditation ❦ Karren L. Alenier . . . 110
A Dog. ❦ Jack and Jill remastered ❦ Julien Berman . . . 112
A White Hunter. ❦ flywheel in America ❦ Karren L. Alenier . . . 114
A Leave. ❦ after "A Leave" ❦ Rae Armantrout . . . 116
Suppose An Eyes. ❦ suppose ❦ Carolyne Wright . . . 118
A Shawl ❦ a caul is not a shawl ❦ Barbara Goldberg . . . 120
Book. ❦ no book. ❦ Margo Taft Stever . . . 122
Peeled Pencil, Choke. ❦ from the belly: a dialectic ❦ Karren L. Alenier . . . 124
It Was Black, Black Took. ❦ blackened was ❦ Brad Richard . . . 126
This Is This Dress, Aider. ❦ having words: a round ❦ Karren L. Alenier . . . 128

Appendix A: How Does One Read Tender Buttons? . . . 131

Appendix B: Ways for Invoking the Steinian Muse . . . 134

Contributor Biographies . . . 135

Index (by Author) . . . 140

Introduction

by Karren L. Alenier

Forget work—this is your invitation to play. What is play? What is the purpose of play? How does something playful improve our sense of wellbeing? Words that come to mind: recreation, creation, acting, interacting, gaming, sporting, laughing, joking, teasing, experimentation, thinking outside the box. Results of playing might include stress reduction, new learning, sharper thinking, increased energy, happier relationships.

In the late 1970s, I felt Gertrude Stein's invitation to play when I read her book with the amusing title *The Autobiography of Alice B. Toklas*. At that time, I set my poem "Leo on Seesaw" on a child's playground which I, as an adult, wanting that irrepressible energy, rapidly claimed for myself.

LEO ON SEESAW

*for the pleasure
of Gertrude Stein*

Little Buddha   little brooder
Kleiner Bruder   tiny brother
bitty bother   sitting baldly
in the butter   in the batter
     shaking philosophic digits
         in the kitchen
         for the Kuchen
         has been eaten
         by the kitten
wearing mittens   in the winter
hiding splinters   in his fingers
         finding spiders
         in the cracks
         of the plaster
         So we laughed
     twenty HA HA HA HA HA
       in metered breathing
         something close
         to the day
         he was born

After Professor Al Filreis went public on Coursera in 2012 with his class Modern & American Contemporary Poetry (ModPo), I decided to lead discussions on Gertrude Stein's *Tender Buttons* within his discussion forums. Published in 1914, this one-of-a-kind work is a book-length poem divided into three sections—OBJECTS, FOOD, ROOMS—and may be a love poem and the marriage contract between Gertrude Stein and her life-long partner Alice Babette Toklas. If so, the agreement was that, as a clandestine married couple, their offspring would be books conceived by Stein. This is one way of looking at *Tender Buttons*.

The upshot was I wrote many poems inspired by the subpoems of Stein's most mysterious work. Later I decided to share with others this opportunity to play. Why not take my own advice not to go into the Steinian woods alone? So the first run of poems in response to Stein's "Objects" (section one of *Tender Buttons*) are mine, but help was soon on the way.

I invited thirty-six poets, teachers, or students of ModPo to react, to free associate with the "objects"—subpoems—of the first section of *Tender Buttons*. I shared with them poems I had written in reaction to the tender objects, and randomly assigned each invité(e) a subpoem for their consideration from the "Objects" section. In *this* book, the poems whose titles appear in caps, those, for the most part, on the left-hand pages, are the original "Objects" by Stein, using the same order in which they appeared in the 1914 edition of *Tender Buttons*. Following each object, its own title in plain Roman text, is the response by a poet, whose name appears at its conclusion.

Some of their poems and mine spring from a variety of creative impulses or inputs—interpretive (expanding on Stein's words), language play, fantasias, current events, exploration and measurement of earthly space, high and low culture, Stein's biography and historical events of her time, Stein's published work, art and design, philosophy or something else contrary to Stein, possibly a spin-off. Thus, this collection sings with poetic experiments ranging from comic to serious, poems that I hope will slow down your reading of Stein's *Tender Buttons* and open up new worlds and new ways of experiencing poetry, especially the poetry of Gertrude Stein.

—Karren LaLonde Alenier

Many interpretive readings of *Tender Buttons* are possible. In that spirit, we invite you, the reader, to enter this work as a playground—to let your own imagination respond to Stein's willful and whimsical disruptions or to the responding poet's juicy reply, or any wild imitation or transgression or combination of both. Please fill the white spaces here with your own words. Let our words play together.

Participation is a requirement for reading Stein. She invites you to get out your magnifying glass, to tune up your singing voice, to play Scrabble with her letters, to read what she has written through a kaleidoscope, to take out your perfume and be intoxicated.

So there is space here for you to enter. No poetry should be impenetrable. No poem shuts you out unless you permit it to do so. You own all the words. This book is yours.

When you enter the Steinian woods, take all your family, friends, and acolytes. The more the merrier.

V 1
OBJECTS

A CARAFE, THAT IS A BLIND GLASS.

A kind in glass and a cousin, a spectacle and nothing strange a single hurt color and an arrangement in a system to pointing. All this and not ordinary, not unordered in not resembling. The difference is spreading.

on the matter of being
3 February 1874

in a window
in or around
Pittsburgh
she comes to
stress matters
stress matters
in the slide
between inside
and out
is she dreaming
or being dreamt
I dream   you
dream   she
dreams   they
dream dreamed
dreamt
the *t* versus
ed irregular
past tense
or living
verb
the British
channel
between
learn and
spill
still
what matters
the interior
smaller or larger
than the cell

—*Karren L. Alenier*

GLAZED GLITTER.

Nickel, what is nickel, it is originally rid of a cover.

The change in that is that red weakens an hour. The change has come. There is no search. But there is, there is that hope and that interpretation and sometime, surely any s is unwelcome, sometime there is breath and there will be a sinecure and charming very charming is that clean and cleansing. Certainly glittering is handsome and convincing.

There is no gratitude in mercy and in medicine. There can be breakages in Japanese. That is no programme. That is no color chosen. It was chosen yesterday, that showed spitting and perhaps washing and polishing. It certainly showed no obligation and perhaps if borrowing is not natural there is some use in giving.

making Americans

soil
toil

seed
feed

male
female

fluency
currency

her story
his story

mystery
history

breath
death

—*Karren L. Alenier*

A SUBSTANCE IN A CUSHION.

The change of color is likely and a difference a very little difference is prepared. Sugar is not a vegetable.

Callous is something that hardening leaves behind what will be soft if there is a genuine interest in there being present as many girls as men. Does this change. It shows that dirt is clean when there is a volume.

A cushion has that cover. Supposing you do not like to change, supposing it is very clear that there is no change in appearance, supposing that there is regularity and a costume is that any the worse than an oyster and an exchange. Come to season that is there any extreme use in feathers and cotton. Is there not much more joy in a table and more chairs and very likely roundness and a place to put them.

A circle of fine card board and a chance to see a tassel.

What is the use of a violent kind of delightfulness if there is no pleasure in not getting tired of it. The question does not come before there is a quotation. In any kind of place there is a top to covering and it is a pleasure at any rate there is some venturing in refusing to believe nonsense. It shows what use there is in a whole piece if one uses it and it is extreme and very likely the little things could be dearer but in any case there is a bargain and if there is the best thing to do is to take it away and wear it and then be reckless be reckless and resolved on returning gratitude.

Light blue and the same red with purple makes a change. It shows that there is no mistake. Any pink shows that and very likely it is reasonable. Very likely there should not be a finer fancy present. Some increase means a calamity and this is the best preparation for three and more being together. A little calm is so ordinary and in any case there is sweetness and some of that.

A seal and matches and a swan and ivy and a suit.

A closet, a closet does not connect under the bed. The band if it is white and black, the band has a green string. A sight a whole sight and a little groan grinding makes a trimming such a sweet singing trimming and a red thing not a round thing but a white thing, a red thing and a white thing.

The disgrace is not in carelessness nor even in sewing it comes out out of the way.

What is the sash like. The sash is not like anything mustard it is not like a same thing that has stripes, it is not even more hurt than that, it has a little top.

the worthy one

see Daddy a beauty
Daddy a beauty beautiful
butterfly and the beetles
are dark dark and shiny
perfectly pinned
to the board the hard
part finding a worthy
one worthy to collect
worthy to see Daddy
you frown what
cruel the pleasure
of killing—the collecting
a cruel killing of what is
worthy what is beautiful
what is sorry so sorry
Daddy I'll stop stop now
good night forgive me
I'll sleep I won't cheat
nature   no pleasure
to collect dead things
tomorrow I'll be
the good son

my son dream of dreams
the wings of the butterfly
are still the beautiful wings
still as a photograph locked in
time my son my life given
flight   cruel—the killing of
this winged thing what is
the pleasure of collecting
the beautiful dead
                  my son
my shotgun seed sown one night in
your mother's womb
                  —my slippery
sperm like a shiny beetle
invading the dew-wet rose—
sleep now and oh
there goes the perfect one   how to catch
that velvety white one there got it
got the moth for my son to keep   am I not
a good father

—*Karren L. Alenier*

A BOX.

Out of kindness comes redness and out of rudeness comes rapid same question, out of an eye comes research, out of selection comes painful cattle. So then the order is that a white way of being round is something suggesting a pin and is it disappointing, it is not, it is so rudimentary to be analysed and see a fine substance strangely, it is so earnest to have a green point not to red but to point again.

the wars of Leo Stein

to Europe came the Great
War no one believed
the years it would consume
Leo fought his indigestion
anxiety need for love if he
was annoyed with Gertrude's
sisterly choice Alice could only
be introduced as secretary—
even that word suggested the lie
their lying together

no secret about Nina
of Montparnasse an artist model a
sleep-around he filled his desires
honestly openly he could marry
Nina quit the prostitutes make a
real marriage unlike his Japanese
wife of only three months but Nina's
brothers one killed the other two
wounded so she left their nest in
Settignano for Paris and he on whim

sailed spring 1915 from Genoa for the
States the pleasurable commerce of
friends and family two operations for
fistulas Kellogg cereal cures a new set
of analysts who said he must have sex
he wrote Nina we have missed our
moment then she must join him but
submarines sank the Lusitania better
to be thin on rations than to die at sea
Leo's German father keeping him from love

—*Karren L. Alenier*

A PIECE OF COFFEE.

More of double.

A place in no new table.

A single image is not splendor. Dirty is yellow. A sign of more in not mentioned. A piece of coffee is not a detainer. The resemblance to yellow is dirtier and distincter. The clean mixture is whiter and not coal color, never more coal color than altogether.

The sight of a reason, the same sight slighter, the sight of a simpler negative answer, the same sore sounder, the intention to wishing, the same splendor, the same furniture.

The time to show a message is when too late and later there is no hanging in a blight.

A not torn rose-wood color. If it is not dangerous then a pleasure and more than any other if it is cheap is not cheaper. The amusing side is that the sooner there are no fewer the more certain is the necessity dwindled. Supposing that the case contained rose wood and a color. Supposing that there was no reason for a distress and more likely for a number, supposing that there was no astonishment, is it not necessary to mingle astonishment.

The settling of stationing cleaning is one way not to shatter scatter and scattering. The one way to use custom is to use soap and silk for cleaning. The one way to see cotton is to have a design concentrating the illusion and the illustration. The perfect way is to accustom the thing to have a lining and the shape of a ribbon and to be solid, quite solid in standing and to use heaviness in morning. It is light enough in that. It has that shape nicely. Very nicely may not be exaggerating. Very strongly may be sincerely fainting. May be strangely flattering. May not be strange in everything. May not be strange to.

herd speak: a reflection

> *Poets love love. We're sated by what seems.*
> *Then unlike chatterers who speak in herds,*
> *We seek the best of all possible…words.*
> —The Metromaniacs

Gertrude Stein and Alice Toklas kaffeeklatsched
they spoke in rippling ribbon code.
What is a tender button but a nipple a calf
knows well on his mother's udder. Who speaks
cow in Voltaire's best of all possible…
Was it Candide? Indeed, Alice Babette Toklas
served the best Sunday roast beef she
eschewed British mutton in favor of Monday's
Boeuf Bourguignon cubes of boneless
meat browned in three tablespoons of lard
several ounces of salt pork a dozen
tiny onions a dollop of flour two
cups of very old dry Burgundy redder
than blood garlic then a bouquet
of orange peel bay leaf sprig of thyme
sliver of nutmeg salt but never never
pepper. How poets pine among
pines. How they play at plays.

—Karren L. Alenier

DIRT AND NOT COPPER.

Dirt and not copper makes a color darker. It makes the shape so heavy and makes no melody harder. It makes mercy and relaxation and even a strength to spread a table fuller. There are more places not empty. They see cover.

the entrance: a count off in eights

the kitchen is shredding it dis
poses the reed slender leaved stalk
tall in evening light shorter in
difference imputes clacking beads
like chickens that fight like soaping
cups queer to slight slippery as
flat porcelain sweeter then fat
a flute without flirt so tone deaf

—*Karren L. Alenier*

NOTHING ELEGANT.

A charm a single charm is doubtful. If the red is rose and there is a gate surrounding it, if inside is let in and there places change then certainly something is upright. It is earnest.

about the word

the pen is the
pen is an organ
flaccid or sound

muscular music
flowing milk or ink
Horace said pen

is tongue of
mind who needs
articles point is

pen is maker
of kind teacher
teaching us

right

       —*Karren L. Alenier*

MILDRED'S UMBRELLA.

A cause and no curve, a cause and loud enough, a cause and extra a loud clash and an extra wagon, a sign of extra, a sac a small sac and an established color and cunning, a slender grey and no ribbon, this means a loss a great loss a restitution.

umbrella suite: a gauge

I. revenge

first the umbrella
stuffy spiney fella
she dragged through
the morning mud
inside her gut
spud of dirty loss
the other school
kids leaving her
behind short legs
not keeping up
bumbershoot a
silky bloom in rain
in snow now no
canopy no cone
of care dare she
shout who would
hear she beat
the soft ground
splashing filthy
her shoes her
socks her shins
over and over
she sang out *I
will throw it in
the mud* then
she did

II. retribution

on the way walking
to the singing coach
strategy for reaching
high notes playing
replaying in her mind
ah   she opened her
rosebud mouth   ah
a man handling an
umbrella like a club
a woman shrieking
under his blows he
warning *leave me
alone* she crying
help me you must
the girl stopped
short resolved to
go straight to
college not let
any man hold
an umbrella
over her head

—Karren L. Alenier

A METHOD OF A CLOAK.

A single climb to a line, a straight exchange to a cane, a desperate adventure and courage and a clock, all this which is a system, which has feeling, which has resignation and success, all makes an attractive black silver.

taken for a ride

cluck cloak clock
clang bang rang

 two belle brains
chucking corsets
removing
pantaloons
petticoats
high button boots

only time
ticking time
in the saddle
could buck her
off was she fly
was she prig

cluck cloak clock
clang bang rang

 —*Karren L. Alenier*

A RED STAMP.

If lilies are lily white if they exhaust noise and distance and even dust, if they dusty will dirt a surface that has no extreme grace, if they do this and it is not necessary it is not at all necessary if they do this they need a catalogue.

whiff

summer soup with celery
intercut the white
lily bulb sweet
crunch more
intense than
water chestnut
my bride's bouquet
a yin to my yearning

—*Karren L. Alenier*

A BOX.

A large box is handily made of what is necessary to replace any substance. Suppose an example is necessary, the plainer it is made the more reason there is for some outward recognition that there is a result.

A box is made sometimes and them to see to see to it neatly and to have the holes stopped up makes it necessary to use paper.

A custom which is necessary when a box is used and taken is that a large part of the time there are three which have different connections. The one is on the table. The two are on the table. The three are on the table. The one, one is the same length as is shown by the cover being longer. The other is different there is more cover that shows it. The other is different and that makes the corners have the same shade the eight are in singular arrangement to make four necessary.

Lax, to have corners, to be lighter than some weight, to indicate a wedding journey, to last brown and not curious, to be wealthy, cigarettes are established by length and by doubling.

Left open, to be left pounded, to be left closed, to be circulating in summer and winter, and sick color that is grey that is not dusty and red shows, to be sure cigarettes do measure an empty length sooner than a choice in color.

Winged, to be winged means that white is yellow and pieces pieces that are brown are dust color if dust is washed off, then it is choice that is to say it is fitting cigarettes sooner than paper.

An increase why is an increase idle, why is silver cloister, why is the spark brighter, if it is brighter is there any result, hardly more than ever.

a box

Even unfilled a box
contains inside-
out-opening
amorphously

as an untethered "a"
[as in "a" pack of cigarettes
unwrapped in a bed
alone in a room].

A list, personal belongings
from a box, as if all is
accounted for [a silver
lighter, a folded blouse, etc.]

Or else uneventful origami,
wings unfolded leaving
the banality of brown dust
under an unmade bed.

—*Roger Sedarat*

A PLATE.

An occasion for a plate, an occasional resource is in buying and how soon does washing enable a selection of the same thing neater. If the party is small a clever song is in order.

Plates and a dinner set of colored china. Pack together a string and enough with it to protect the center, cause a considerable haste and gather more as it is cooling, collect more trembling and not any even trembling, cause a whole thing to be a church.

A sad size a size that is not sad is blue as every bit of blue is precocious. A kind of green a game in green and nothing flat nothing quite flat and more round, nothing a particular color strangely, nothing breaking the losing of no little piece.

A splendid address a really splendid address is not shown by giving a flower freely, it is not shown by a mark or by wetting.

Cut cut in white, cut in white so lately. Cut more than any other and show it. Show it in the stem and in starting and in evening coming complication.

A lamp is not the only sign of glass. The lamp and the cake are not the only sign of stone. The lamp and the cake and the cover are not the only necessity altogether.

A plan a hearty plan, a compressed disease and no coffee, not even a card or a change to incline each way, a plan that has that excess and that break is the one that shows filling.

temple and tiger

Waking from a frilled dream, Rousseau
Asks his bride, the tiger, where's the trousseau?
Ask the panther, the tigress says. The panther growls,
"Clouseau!" Clouseau suggests the dress, the scene,
Require the presence of a real McQueen.
The big cats in their feathered boas
Come and go. Nobody speaks of Michelangelo.

The French are hampered by subjunctive mood.
They look for food and laundresses. Antoinette's
Powdered tress spills into a basket. An antique,
The Lion King declares! A trasket case! Question
Talleyrand. We're on it, the detectives say. Nothing is detected.
Rien. It has been around forever. The Ancien Rien. A round
Forever round about.

Have a quick look at figure and ground, burps the historiographer.
The Scrovegni panels, say. Like in trays, fish and figures flounder
from them. Anne's man puckers for the first kiss, faithfully cuckolded,
Nobody can explain how, yet. Love is love is love.
Leaping from the print, the page. Intaglio. Oh! How they saw it.
It figures. Feet hard upon the ground. Joint bearing on joint
Until we get to the hands and the hands holding

Plates. Crowns. Like dentists: masters of porcelain. To eat from a plate
You need this plate, Pavlov relates, years later. And the musicians
Play. It's a dance thing. A knee—jerk reaction. More cowbell,
Says the engineer. Pretty please the psychologist parrots.
We're drooling all over and over again. Again and again.
World without end. Round and about. From the first fig leaf
Of trousseau to the last. At the chapel's other end

The devil's arrowed tail pierces ass and scrotum. Who wants
To have a party now? Pretty please Polly says. Nein! The next
War shouts. None of it. We'll have none of it at all. But cake,
Perhaps? In the basket? A miracle for the party, like the loaves
And fishes. Go ask the oaf for a loaf. And the smith for a fish.
Somebody will come back with a windvane that points the wrong way.
Tail headed upstream. Well smithed, but lazy fish. Going

With the flow. Out to Pasteur. Coming in from the lawn when called
For milking. But it is milting that makes milk happen.
Milting all over. The sea. The promissory fountains and rainbows
Chock full, as Eugenius Philalethes said, of seed. Not egg.
Descending in torrent. Danae's gold. "The first sperm and matter
Of the world." From that garden, with its feast laid out like fortune's
Cards upon the baize, the chips stacked in the corners, the guests

Awaiting the display of the sheet. There is no telling,
So soon after the conjugation. Figure and ground.
Far above the great mother and her cuckold consort, Giotto's
Empyrean rests as the ancients thought it must, in the home
Of the fixed stars. The already counted cards. The plates
Upon which the half-eaten sandwiches of the world rest.
Carried along in the plasterer's cerulean blue and twinkling
gilt. Restored. Briefly glimpsed. Forever out of reach.

—*Michael Davis*

A SELTZER BOTTLE.

Any neglect of many particles to a cracking, any neglect of this makes around it what is lead in color and certainly discolor in silver. The use of this is manifold. Supposing a certain time selected is assured, suppose it is even necessary, suppose no other extract is permitted and no more handling is needed, suppose the rest of the message is mixed with a very long slender needle and even if it could be any black border, supposing all this altogether made a dress and suppose it was actual, suppose the mean way to state it was occasional, if you suppose this in August and even more melodiously, if you suppose this even in the necessary incident of there certainly being no middle in summer and winter, suppose this and an elegant settlement a very elegant settlement is more than of consequence, it is not final and sufficient and substituted. This which was so kindly a present was constant.

trinken aus "A Seltzer Bottle."

picking at particles
looking up this
looking up that
hearing seltzer
spec-u-la-ting the sonic
boom the sound energy
bubble wake of
carbonate pop pop
message mixed with a
probe stippled says
the printer dot dot
black at the border
the dress added as after-
thought more address as
in to speak into speech
all so kindly present
no kindly constant
genug bitte Wasser
ohne geschmäckern

  —Karren L. Alenier

A LONG DRESS.

What is the current that makes machinery, that makes it crackle, what is the current that presents a long line and a necessary waist. What is this current.

What is the wind, what is it.

Where is the serene length, it is there and a dark place is not a dark place, only a white and red are black, only a yellow and green are blue, a pink is scarlet, a bow is every color. A line distinguishes it. A line just distinguishes it.

birth of the long dress made in America

What is the current that makes machinery.

from the union
of the needle
threaded with
cotton or silk
union of
needle head in
socket of the
machine machine
joined to the
current of a
woman's nether
limbs feet on the
treadle pumping
clacking her
fingers push
blue or red
cloth under
pulsing
point of steel
bellows of the
boss breathing
hot wind on
delicate necks
her sisters in
unison the close
quarters locked
into the business
of long hours
long days becoming

—Karren L. Alenier

A RED HAT.

A dark grey, a very dark grey, a quite dark grey is monstrous ordinarily, it is so monstrous because there is no red in it. If red is in everything it is not necessary. Is that not an argument for any use of it and even so is there any place that is better, is there any place that has so much stretched out.

a red hat

there we lay
stretched out
beneath red cumulus
surrendering to the leviathan
    cloaked in grey shroud
yet filled with light

— *Harold M. Greenwald*

A BLUE COAT.

A blue coat is guided guided away, guided and guided away, that is the particular color that is used for that length and not any width not even more than a shadow.

a blue coat

whether gendarme
one arm extended
ended by white glove uni-

form a length of sky in
eye cerulean coast Côte
d'Azure sea and land

fractal lines into in-
finity a dark closet
for custom cloaks

nope petit bleu
blown through tubes
pneumatique freaky

jokey pornography
covers all blue
singing a—b—c

    —Karren L. Alenier

A PIANO.

If the speed is open, if the color is careless, if the event is overtaken, if the selection of a strong scent is not awkward, if the button holder is held by all the waving color and there is no color, not any color. If there is no dirt in a pin and there can be none scarcely, if there is not then the place is the same as up standing.

This is no dark custom and it even is not acted in any such a way that a restraint is not spread. That is spread, it shuts and it lifts and awkwardly not awkwardly the center is in standing.

an open piano

It was the day
      I noticed the mustard jar squatting heavy
      on the refrigerator shelf. The day
I looked up the word 'awkwardly' in our blue
      promiscuous dictionary. Yes,
it was the day I noticed my socks running
      out of thread so I called upstairs for a hand.
That day. The one when the telephone was let off the hook
      and almonds broke out all over us. The
very day I handed you my driver's license
      and took your glass of warm refreshing milk
      in a careless never-ceasing way. You know, that
day. The time I heard a sound like a salon
      coming out of our living room.
The day I looked in to see the black enameled cover
      lifted off the piano and keys exploding
      all over your finite grin. That day
when nothing stood between us.

      —*Henry Crawford*

A CHAIR.

A widow in a wise veil and more garments shows that shadows are even. It addresses no more, it shadows the stage and learning. A regular arrangement, the severest and the most preserved is that which has the arrangement not more than always authorised.

A suitable establishment, well housed, practical, patient and staring, a suitable bedding, very suitable and not more particularly than complaining, anything suitable is so necessary.

A fact is that when the direction is just like that, no more, longer, sudden and at the same time not any sofa, the main action is that without a blaming there is no custody.

Practice measurement, practice the sign that means that really means a necessary betrayal, in showing that there is wearing.

Hope, what is a spectacle, a spectacle is the resemblance between the circular side place and nothing else, nothing else.

To choose it is ended, it is actual and more than that it has it certainly has the same treat, and a seat all that is practiced and more easily much more easily ordinarily.

Pick a barn, a whole barn, and bend more slender accents than have ever been necessary, shine in the darkness necessarily.

Actually not aching, actually not aching, a stubborn bloom is so artificial and even more than that, it is a spectacle, it is a binding accident, it is animosity and accentuation.

If the chance to dirty diminishing is necessary, if it is why is there no complexion, why is there no rubbing, why is there no special protection.

the entire text is a field

A gleaning, after a harvest of any kind, is that which lays bare the labor and the luck. Almanacs fail us. Medical celebrities fail us. Cruise lines, surfaces, cheap screws too. Have you heard the one about the plowman and the weather? His blood pressure kept matching the air's until, like fragrant smoke leaving a thurible, *poof* he was suddenly in everyone's clothes. So pick a field, a whole field, and observe the precise degree at which the heaviest sustenance hangs. Someone I know decided upon poppies, an endless distance of them, heavy-lidded on their own product. Of course, you must also select a chair, any chair, and put it in that field. I placed a La-Z-Boy in an acre of cane, late summer, all those sweet bodies going gold in the setting sun, laid back and saw sky, a graffiti-blue being scissored by the contrail of a G6, a single attendant with a moment dreaming down.   A chair says it's not a table by suddenly deciding to go vertical. A field says *I can be anything I damn well please*. Pablo's a genius or an incorrigible asshole drawing another hand for Alice to needlepoint the shit out of, stunningly, exquisitely, so selflessly into a Louis XV chair that everyone is certain they now know what tenderness is. Everyone is alive and asking for answers, so many voices at once comprised wholly of the hollows of throats. To be everywhere, to be nowhere, to be where there is no there. But why so many choose a cordoned off chair in some museum's quiet air, in its inoffensive light is a mystery. No one's sitting in that chair, nor permitted to, a terrible shame given its form was made to bear the weight of us.

—Nils Michals

A FRIGHTFUL RELEASE.

A bag which was left and not only taken but turned away was not found. The place was shown to be very like the last time. A piece was not exchanged, not a bit of it, a piece was left over. The rest was mismanaged.

the bag dreams

rightful ease
           A was
    not taken
           but found
   lace was how
           time
changed
           not a bit of it
was managed

   *****

not taken   [for a purse]
exchange as   [contagion]

[no dreaming peerless]

   *****

A fo(u)nd
rest

   —Burgi Zenhaeusern

A PURSE.

A purse was not green, it was not straw color, it was hardly seen and it had a use a long use and the chain, the chain was never missing, it was not misplaced, it showed that it was open, that is all that it showed.

two more purses

When my mother passed, I emptied her white purse—
tissue pack and reading glasses, coupons
and address book. I once lived in the purse
inside her, my first pink home, the knotted strap
an umbilical cord. When I grew up, I took care
of my own purse, its pristine lining, never stretched
or stuffed with a fetus. I waxed the buckles,
polished the pink clit, the tender button that opened
and closed my clutch. I carried pleasure inside me,
my lips keeping so many secrets.
I tipped my mother's empty purse upside down,
its vulnerable silk insides torn.

—Denise Duhamel

A MOUNTED UMBRELLA.

What was the use of not leaving it there where it would hang what was the use if there was no chance of ever seeing it come there and show that it was handsome and right in the way it showed it. The lesson is to learn that it does show it, that it shows it and that nothing, that there is nothing, that there is no more to do about it and just so much more is there plenty of reason for making an exchange.

returning to the father

because Martha offered
her father sugar
when he wanted
only the blackest
black in his cup…
because her Phillip
used his Martha up,
tossed his wife aside
in favor of a greater
intellect—he embraced
change what was that
other woman's name
because she was stuck
like a gold ring unable
to skirt an old bride's
knuckle the morality
of pain claimed her
dug in like an army
of bed bugs after
his boss told Martha
to control her husband—
what she lost her
umbrella one he would
never hold they had no
son or daughter she
was speechless—but
he left anyway then he died
young and joyfully while she
denied every thing and held
out the sugar bowl and silver
spoon to cut the bitterness
in her father's daily dose
of aromatic brew the aged
man had to face it—his fortune
was spent

—*Karren L. Alenier*

A CLOTH.

Enough cloth is plenty and more, more is almost enough for that and besides if there is no more spreading is there plenty of room for it. Any occasion shows the best way.

rare on rares

As rags do for clearing hearts—
       how float or folds or frayings will
       this woo but dust
            as cotton loves.

These wifely husband also years
       spread from where to there
            with every why and might
       in knotted-patterned overlays
            all as if
            if has come.

How threaded throughs are woven less—
       how hardly clings
            to plenty's fringe of cares
       then rare on rares
       how wonder-spills
            best wipe and way.

       —*Hiram Larew*

MORE.

An elegant use of foliage and grace and a little piece of white cloth and oil.

Wondering so winningly in several kinds of oceans is the reason that makes red so regular and enthusiastic. The reason that there is more snips are the same shining very colored rid of no round color.

less

I do not want to mirror you Gertrude, turn the Mississippi back to the future as the hurricane Ida achieved, current turning negative, not flowing to the ocean but engulfing land that once was ocean this bizarre new world in which we live almost one hundred years after you wrote MORE, we are burrowing deeply into LESS. LESS vertebrates. LESS trees....but yet we have water. everywhere. MORE MORE. And fire. blazing MORE MORE.

—*Indran Amirthanayagam*

A NEW CUP AND SAUCER.

Enthusiastically hurting a clouded yellow bud and saucer, enthusiastically so is the bite in the ribbon.

entwine

To be the roundness of the bowl and the bowl itself.
Container of words, ideas, overflow
knowing Alice would be there, to receive your
brilliance and open it to the world.

Every plate, cup and saucer have a function,
a duty if only to simply revel in the dance of the divine.
Elegant under life yours secreted between you
against the gritty predictability of the conventional.

Whom needed who more?
Blazing moment Gertrude met you for the first time.
Having recognized each other in new forms.
This soul gaze, like the meeting of Shams and Rumi.

Paris where you two walked the labyrinth
going from stranger to friend. The golden
thread Alice carried charged you so much,
you would follow it to your dying breath.

What was the answer you sought in each other?
Alice protected the yellow bud blossom, never
letting artists, men or other women stay for too long.
Knew better than Ariadne, never to sleep away the days ahead.

Some thought your aspiration was art making,
cultivating its twisted lit cord in others.
To create a new, blur reality, upend lines.
Joy gift of a lifetime.

— *Jacqueline Johnson*

OBJECTS.

Within, within the cut and slender joint alone, with sudden equals and no more than three, two in the center make two one side.

If the elbow is long and it is filled so then the best example is all together.

The kind of show is made by squeezing.

to not OBJECTify

What is a spectacle if not magnified as show. A woman's waist less than a span. So the touch is show, a squeeze to show ripeness and complicity. The table is less than. The body moves and alters, the body is an object. Stand still and slender or stable here. Why not embrace across the glass and silver. Say butter, say what now.

With and within, both-withy, with or without, wit, with who, with what, with, in with, whither, within, within the cut. Would this be next. Alone and with, inside, a side, one side, in the center why. Why within a wound a slender cut.

[she writes with a scissor-shaped instrument, she cuts into the body of language.]

One is one and all alone, alone and together, two a side. In the beginning three and not two. Mathematics is play and play is language.

How she fills my elbow, how she falls into the curve of an arm, how the crook of an elbow is filled and for show. The best example. No more than. We are all sudden equals.

The kind of show goes on. The kind we know. Raise no objects, no objections. A slender joint pared clean of meat. The cut goes deep. So then swaying we might begin, the long-limbed have it. Three are two in one, she in me, the other at her elbow, the two across the table. Say now.

[could she measure opacity. Did she love may and helen and were they all present for show. Did she count the embraces. Cream squeezed onto red jam, the sweet strawberry jam on a side plate. The way she carved the joint, head of the household at the table, so then her cut within the slender joint. Might two be best or three or two across and each side has two or a center, a middle place.]

They were all together at the table and sudden equals they knew best. The object of the show was to divide and come together, to add to what was filled and the best example. When what is solid yields to squeezing, What is filled and not enough, enough for now. To bend is flexible, the table is fixed, numbers pair off as geese or condiments. Grease on the counterpane, the differences too numerous, the words that take their place. Here is the century unbuttoning as new. Here is a new century, buttered and sliced open. What is missing. What is surplus and will carry on.

[her small handwriting as cursive on the page, from carnet to copy to be typed by another, to count words in each line, as print to obviate the center]

—Mary Armour

EYE GLASSES.

A color in shaving, a saloon is well placed in the center of an alley.

a Steinian stethoscope

some like
the being
they have
in them—but what if
they are sick stuck
in their middle
living with frightening
illness some can
tell what way
being is inside
in men in women
at sixty fifty forty-five
forty thirty twenty-eight
twenty-two eighteen four-
teen eleven seven five
three one less I am
learning what counts
in eating sleeping moving
talking all of living before
one becomes a
dead one

—*Karren L. Alenier*

A CUTLET.

A blind agitation is manly and uttermost.

portrait of the father

inside him a big
feeling big Arabian
nights drama more
than talking and listening
forget snacking a banquet
of tales to keep him
alive chewing with new
vigor what could she
say to fill his feeling
all his theories—
living eating dying—
this pit of sadness
this fear leading to
the end

—*Karren L. Alenier*

CARELESS WATER.

No cup is broken in more places and mended, that is to say a plate is broken and mending does do that it shows that culture is Japanese. It shows the whole element of angels and orders. It does more to choosing and it does more to that ministering counting. It does, it does change in more water.

Supposing a single piece is a hair supposing more of them are orderly, does that show that strength, does that show that joint, does that show that balloon famously. Does it.

when you sit down to.
write it down to.
bless it for.

unrequited is.
only yet for.
him or her looking.

this is when.
begging water to.
crawl on.
tongue and skin and.

bodies then.
alone all up in.

I am because.
when you turn to.
this is wanting when.

I still.
blessing only and.

   —Nikia Chaney

A PAPER.

A courteous occasion makes a paper show no such occasion and this makes readiness and eyesight and likeness and a stool.

(rock) paper (scissors)

Carte d'identité   stolen   in the warren (under)   Grand Central   six months
(permission)   left

Rolled-up certificate in a car   trunk (from Stein's time)   in a language
/font/type-face   hard to read   where she learns   she is
not   who she thought   she/they/he was

The small white card   that tells the world   X received two shots
at Dodger Stadium   Long lines snaking   no (hot)dogs

Mrs. Blair's Brownies   in Palmer script short   hand for butter
translated   at the margin tempting   to leave them too long   in
A leap of faith to know they will be tender   (when [barely] set)

In a trolley   conductor's home   after the Spanish   flu. "Poor Man's Cake"
with newfangled vegetable   shortening (not lard),   molasses, Muskat
almost impossible   to find dear glacéed cherries   ringing the diminutive ring

Her writing, like (mine) the knob   on an index   finger from gripping   a pen,
the knuckle at the base swollen like (hers)

How many pages pens ran   dry   in how many   languages. Paper
gives (meaning),   records,   accompanies.

Two dozen certified Death   Certificates the end   paper bookends   birth
(Fraktur), Ketubah (marriage),   the deed   to the family plot filled
in over a hundred years   waiting

                    Two empty spaces left   the last
words   a long line   cut, another   matching stone with matching square
periods instead of commas   raised in granite   stones at their heads   Rock
Paper Scissors   Stein   Papier   Cisseaux   Scissors Rock   Paper

—*Andrea Carter Brown*

A DRAWING.

The meaning of this is entirely and best to say the mark, best to say it best to show sudden places, best to make bitter, best to make the length tall and nothing broader, anything between the half.

the story ands (this is how)

The end of ampersand is and, remember.
The rock face, the moon face, the lead face.
The and of krugerrand is to be a microinfluencer, remember.
The end of remember is amber, ampere, amplify, amplified.
The making of a mark is a remarking. Remember.
The mountain face, the forest face, the earth face.
The cat face the bardo face the carousel face the rat year face.
Remember the timbre of member, ember, remember.
Remind me. Remind me in a wing that depends.
On not being in air but beating its fist.
The down to rise. The air face the cloud face the clod.
Place your face in mine. The North Pole face. The Sole face. The breast face.
Draw your face in mine. The fraught face and the frog face. The dole face.
The half-penny face, turning, flicked, spinning on the wood face.
When it is not yet the frog face, not still the tadpole gill face.
In the no-place, let no-place arrive in on itself or let the mark make.
In its own time, let be be the beginning of and.
Let mark be for how can it be otherwise only.
All is Barracuda, Careful, Despoiled, Ernie's and Frog fillings.
Puppet face defaces and then faces to resurface the facts.
The soil is thriving these days – thrilling in the downdraft boom.
Evel Knievel, Bloom Face. Footloose Face.
Garage Salem, the plant face, the shoe face.
The show face, the stunt. The stunted. And drawing you and you in there
Is another letter, a vowel, a ewe face.
Turning so slowly, so slowly, to catch you in.
In the nook at the base of flappering V.
Oh, such a horizontal pupil alphabet.
Isn't it. And your terrible skin, how hold it holds all of you in like a drawing.
So much reach! Such terrible faces you. Never. Remember.

Butterfly. Ands in the meth tongue. Ands in the mouth face.
Drawing itself to say like *open* like to say *re-member* and to like say *re-mouth*.
In the middle of mouth is a drawn out.
A yam face A yawn face, a joy.
To be drawn, A joy to be quartered alive.
So many marks remark a line, a half-faced ace, Ace.
It's all aces. It's all not all wild, but it is not aligned.
The wild face is not on your side and.
You might now like choose. Remember.
To make a like mark, like, it is your choice and.
It cannot be called yours, or like look it can and.

—Jason Zuzga

WATER RAINING.

Water astonishing and difficult altogether makes a meadow and a stroke.

water

The hands of water are feet deep.
The water handle dubbed paddle will betray
the bubble, but don't grow floaty, friend, for if
nipple all swam
the womb, you'd be sorry. Fleeing
the shudder of its over, remember
we were foreign for the first time?

Fast our drop a drowned beneath, oh cradle, and
we don't want to speak it: be in it. A minute
ago I was but now I'm out and fail. You want to say about water
which wastes the shallow. The neighbors say it too and they're gone.

Next year last year, we say, and sink.

Green warns the size, and you
my smash and fluster. Blue the only equidistance.

—*Nancy White*

COLD CLIMATE.

A season in yellow sold extra strings makes lying places.

hat before snow

buttercups face sun
to stay yellow
but since the sun
doesn't know its name
how can it shine
so is the buttercup lying
about color
and then there are those rosebuds
picked too early
who die before blooming
all this because early warmth
deceived the red and pink
so who blames the spirit
of the garden
that grows nevertheless
because of need
or an untruthful sun so
pick flowers make a hat
wear it in the world pretending

—Grace Cavalieri

MALACHITE

The sudden spoon is the same in no size. The sudden spoon is the wound in the decision.

honeycomb

The spoon sits on the windowsill waiting. You hear a tiny wail from the next room. The minutes descend in the blank house. The blankets hold your body back until a cough breaks the silence. You open a door and it is a decision to act but the acting is too late like an actor missing her lines. When you hold the baby the night is an instrument of forgetting. The spoon is too small in its roundness. A shine escapes the baby's mouth. The baby tries to burrow back in. There is no later to capture a comfort. The moment wavers. Your body is a spoon that remembers the carrying.

—Carrie Bennett

AN UMBRELLA.

Coloring high means that the strange reason is in front not more in front behind. Not more in front in peace of the dot.

setting the table

The dining room was awash in color,
the colors suffused with light,
not the morning light
now streaming in
from the kitchen windows,
but rather the light in the paint itself—
the oil, hue, and brushstroke.
Alice didn't understand the paintings.
It was Gertrude who understood,
understood the strange reason
behind them all. But Alice
felt them, their peaceful verve,
their dissonance buzzing
in the room.

Alice set the table and chose
where each painter would sit—
typically facing their own painting.
She knew how to make someone happy.
And was that such a small gift,
after all, making someone happy?
Matisse was coming tonight.
When a Frenchman dined
soufflé would be served.
She was in high color
that morning, covered by color,
an umbrella of colors,
which reminded her
of a painting. She couldn't
recall the title or the painter.
A host of open umbrellas
shimmered in the rain.
At the far end of the street,
a pair of twins, sisters,
shared one umbrella.
Did such a painting exist?
Did she see it once
or did she dream it?

—*Roberto Christiano*

A PETTICOAT.

A light white, a disgrace, an ink spot, a rosy charm.

petticoat

Between me and thee
a seal

My coat of charm

My unbroken pet
hides light
turns glass into
cloud

peek a boo

have a wisp of
steam

Through your petite
department I
rise

Here   now
try this one in
white

stroke un   der   my

knees

      —*JoAnne McFarland*

A WAIST.

A star glide, a single frantic sullenness, a single financial grass greediness.

Object that is in wood. Hold the pine, hold the dark, hold in the rush, make the bottom.

A piece of crystal. A change, in a change that is remarkable there is no reason to say that there was a time.

A wooden object gilded. A country climb is the best disgrace, a couple of practices any of them in order is so left.

in a change that is remarkable there is no reason to say that there was a time

unless with sick child   at last sleeping go on get some

sleep   but won't unless   what had held a violence in place

no less violent in its weak holding   how not to hold a fevered sleeper

is a greenish chill spreading   a splintered time applied

an applied violence to the slenderest strip

of the city not slept in   what has been done becomes

a terminus at a flat center   far from hot bedding   a bosky ardor spied

from satellites   a carob moth flattened

in a mountainous book   opened and never quite closed

on the same page as a fire   as a time to eat   is it time

trapped within the fever dream twitching

watched over look a child in a city inside a country from low orbit

infantile trees planted to keep the dust and cold at bay

burn away to leave where fear's bodice and worry's skirt meet

strictures demanding travel   a way in or

a way applied to the narrowest part of the road out

a gray cargo plane on tarmac   to cling to

a child a way too sick to travel taken

    —*Miles Waggener*

A TIME TO EAT.

A pleasant simple habitual and tyrannical and authorised and educated and resumed and articulate separation. This is not tardy.

gender gluttons

A Time for Two

Pitcher of spoons, tea weapons at the ready, legitimized and stultified, toasted and buttered. This is not lardy.

A Tea to Turn

A season and complex pleasant. Cultivated tyrannosaurus, unauthorized and well-reluméd. This is on the dot.

A Time with Wine

A hobbling sample and tympanical and appetized and elevated and reused and adulterate syncopation. Here's a tawdry article.

A Lime to Sip

A lenient pimple, hospitable and atomized, a particulate and punctual and piquant reparation. This is not despotic.

A Timbale Full

An ample eventual pheasant and tidy and elevated and consumed, an appropriate scintillation. How timely.

—Lillo Way

A LITTLE BIT OF A TUMBLER.

A shining indication of yellow consists in there having been more of the same color than could have been expected when all four were bought. This was the hope which made the six and seven have no use for any more places and this necessarily spread into nothing. Spread into nothing.

the rest of time

A little more than unexpected
having come through

the same yellow, worried
shining and spread low

into nothing that could have been
a fall and so much less

than the etched glass tumblers
weighting our cabinets—

the old mahogany also luminous
and emptied of necessity more

than other places where forsythia
pulled up by the roots and piled up

around hope, a handful, a shovelful,
a little obsessed by words of equal value

like the face his father wore
in the dream there is no language for.

—*Lisa Sewell*

A FIRE.

What was the use of a whole time to send and not send if there was to be the kind of thing that made that come in. A letter was nicely sent.

nicely sent(ient)

A fire.
A fireman.
A fire woman.

A whole.
A whole man.
A whole woman.

The kind of thing that made that.
The kind of thing that made that man.
The kind of thing that made that woman.

Come in. Come in!
Come in, Man.
Come in, Woman.

A whole time to send!

Man.
Woman.
Letter >>>>>>>>>>>>>>>>>>>>>>>>>> SENT
(What was the use?)

Man.
Woman.
Letter <<<<<<<<<<<<<<<<<<<<<<<< UNSENT
(What is the use?)

  —*Bill Yarrow*

A HANDKERCHIEF.

A winning of all the blessings, a sample not a sample because there is no worry.

handkerchief

Kerchief, bandana, hanky,
handmade heirloom lace—
initialed   embroidered   adorned

Sun-shield, bandage or covid-cover,
cloth safeguard
for Itzhak's Stradivarius

Something for absorption
in times of heat, sorrow or disease,
flag of surrender or truce

Intimate object,
disguised token of tenderness—
Desdemona's first gift from Othello

Flirty coded message
depending on color and location
furtive hanky-panky

So here I am with mounds
of outmoded folded fabric
I simply cannot relinquish

Gertrude, my Gertrude,
Grandmother of my heart

—Margery M. Ross

RED ROSES.

A cool red rose and a pink cut pink, a collapse and a sold hole, a little less hot.

rose recipe

melody rose
contradiction
cut pink

nobody's rose
collapse played
seas go dry

sick rose
crimson joy
no one's sleep

easy rose
desire to die
so many lids

warm rose
dark secret love
found out your bed

sold rose
ceases to bloom
only a bee will miss it

white rose
beyond the sun
violets are done

—Donald Illich

IN BETWEEN.

In between a place and candy is a narrow foot path that shows more mounting than anything, so much really that a calling meaning a bolster measured a whole thing with that. A virgin a whole virgin is judged made and so between curves and outlines and real seasons and more out glasses and a perfectly unprecedented arrangement between old ladies and mild colds there is no satin wood shining.

state of the union: a dialectic with "In Between."

In between a place and candy
                                         crush
is a narrow footpath that
                         ran to a sham self-clapping presi-
shows more mounting
                           dent more shame
than anything, so much really that a
                                 stormy
calling meaning a bolster measured
                                  six inches
a whole thing with that.
                         and could it be
A virgin a whole virgin is judged
                                 ass not candy catcher
made and so between
                           soft puta
curves and
            hard cógeme duro
outlines and real
                 ity
seasons and more
                      spies look-
out glasses and a perfectly
                             candy-assed
unprecedented arrangement between old
                                  soldier
ladies and mild
                 wall-less
colds there is no satin
                     sheet no
wood
     pecker
shining.

       —Karren L. Alenier

COLORED HATS.

Colored hats are necessary to show that curls are worn by an addition of blank spaces, this makes the difference between single lines and broad stomachs, the least thing is lightening, the least thing means a little flower and a big delay a big delay that makes more nurses than little women really little women. So clean is a light that nearly all of it shows pearls and little ways. A large hat is tall and me and all custard whole.

colored condoms.

Colored condoms are necessary. They reflect the variety of ways to protect oneself and others from routine and this makes a difference for outies and innies, inclusive terminology for all the bottoms out there. Out there, something else tightens and broad stomachs await the big delay. So lovely the light when it shows a swatch of upstaging skin, and all the custard shades.

—*Kevin McLellan*

A FEATHER.

A feather is trimmed, it is trimmed by the light and the bug and the post, it is trimmed by little leaning and by all sorts of mounted reserves and loud volumes. It is surely cohesive.

the feathered girl

She alights one estival day
like a butterfly kiss
with soft western winds hewing
her sail windward
She soared here
with a rush of soundlessness
and salty light
her plumed journey and its story
of sheltering and defense
intact

—*Martha Sanchez-Lowery*

A BROWN.

A brown which is not liquid not more so is relaxed and yet there is a change, a news is pressing.

pandemic buttons

It was COVID times and we were leaving the city, a news is president threatening to close all the bridges.

We drove into the night and alighted in a still snowy perch upstate where Aaron grew up. A land. More so skies. Which is pastures, water vales, brickyard falls, mill runs, a horizon of cows.

A bleach-soaked rag over the groceries. My in-laws baked the mail. And I pressed mom by phone to stop going to the post office.

It was board games and cards and living room forts. It was pass-the-baton parenting and grading past midnight.

It was months of google meet with ninth grade bubbles. And yet Jacob O doodles on camera an Everett chases his cat. And everyone else writing anxiety and encouragement in the comments. Or there were absences and no-shows and not more logging on. No news. The blues.

A George which is not liquid not more so is relaxed and yet there is a change, a knee is pressing. A brown fence post with rusted barbed wire is overrun by grapevines.

A Bronx is burning again. Ninth graders stuck inside more so. ALL CAPS ANGER. A summer without swimming.

It was a vaccine at the frozen state fairgrounds. Maze of standing, snaking waiting-lines to needles. Bare shouldered fifty-year old posts facebook selfie.

A gray which is a barncat named Romeo. Romeo! The flea-ridden bounty hunter of Broadfield Road, a mews.

A brown cow is braying. Larry says she shouldn't be angry because the calf he gave away was a full grown one-year-old and she was nursing it and was not its mother. The moos are pressing.

—*Amy Feinstein*

A LITTLE CALLED PAULINE.

A little called anything shows shudders.

Come and say what prints all day. A whole few watermelon. There is no pope.

No cut in pennies and little dressing and choose wide soles and little spats really little spices.

A little lace makes boils. This is not true.

Gracious of gracious and a stamp a blue green white bow a blue green lean, lean on the top.

If it is absurd then it is leadish and nearly set in where there is a tight head.

A peaceful life to arise her, moon and moon and moon. A letter a cold sleeve a blanket a shaving house and nearly the best and regular window.

Nearer in fairy sea, nearer and farther, show white has lime in sight, show a stitch of ten. Count, count more so that thicker and thicker is leaning.

I hope she has her cow. Bidding a wedding, widening received treading, little leading, mention nothing.

Cough out cough out in the leather and really feather it is not for.

Please could, please could, jam it not plus more sit in when.

through a little window to the fairy sea

what slows shutters
not air shaving
through louvers

hinges so leadish
lace wings lost
one juice to tend

in country keeping
where known be-
comes noon brighter

than the broil
of white teeth
wedding so many

bows count count
the green lend her
your cow Pauline

throw the pretty
pennies splat
feather leather jam

  —Karren L. Alenier

A SOUND.

Elephant beaten with candy and little pops and chews all bolts and reckless reckless rats, this is this.

SOUND of a SONG for the DOO-DA-DAY

Hypocrisy is a tribute that vice pays to virtue.
—Francois Duc De La Rochefoucauld

Gods, some small,
you weary me, how you goose step
clouds and waves and wars —strutting—

How your reckless rats knife
virtue, no matter her shining
no matter the thisses no matter the thats

How your elephantine spites and violent lies
beat truths with their tongues, and truths with
their bile — till souls spit back —

not candies but blood — not
popping — but
their very quiet deaths.

~

Pied piper for a day
in the get-away woods
where muses and devils bound

Just wait 'til the *piñata* breaks, wait 'til the seas
rise, wait 'til the globe splits in more than two—
or infants howl or heavens reek — Wait.   Just wait.

Whisper : *World in a cell of sand* —   *You'll be alright, just hold on to your flesh—*
Hiss : *You'll be alright, just watch for the ice slopes, falling* — *Wait: for hypocrisy's drowning*   —   *Wait for the sun to burn.*   There are other things that kill.

Trill: World is a world is a world.
Believe in bolts and brass and towers, chewed by rats.
A Piper Pied in satin — who chants *follow me, follow me, do*

to horizon's terminus, *zippedy doo-da,* — believe all the darling day.
Shout: *Follow me zippedy, follow-me—doo-da—follow! to foul the fray.*

Steps be tender, steps be quick, steps be buttoned or un— but beware !
These our darling coming-to-terms days. These our darkling days.

    —Margo Berdeshevsky

A TABLE.

A table means does it not my dear it means a whole steadiness. Is it likely that a change.

A table means more than a glass even a looking glass is tall. A table means necessary places and a revision a revision of a little thing it means it does mean that there has been a stand, a stand where it did shake.

progressively smaller dimensions

You ruined our table
with a sloppy cocktail,
tried to ruin me
with alcohol-sloppy love.
I was already ruined at thirteen
by an older boy I'd never love—
should have known better,
shouldn't have drunk those cocktails,
but I was unstable even then,
and they turned me to stone.
As girls, we liked screwdrivers,
nasty drinks, overly orange,
the non-taste of vodka,
runes for boys priming us
for screwing, with their unbreakable
adolescent cocks. A table
of Picasso-fractals, the destined design
of repeatable patterns.
Look: Our table wobbles.
And you drink too many martinis,
that part is unshakeable.
Nevertheless, I love you.
My love's all very irregular.

—*Susana H. Case*

SHOES.

To be a wall with a damper a stream of pounding way and nearly enough choice makes a steady midnight. It is pus.

A shallow hole rose on red, a shallow hole in and in this makes ale less. It shows shine.

shoe: a *Tender Buttons* meditation

shoe I worry
about shine
the dust the
mark tattoo
on my character
how will the foot
foot the bill
the sharp point
blunt it blunt
let the toes
wiggle in air
let the toes
shape the leather
God, make it leather
buttery as a lamb
give me a horn
to shout *hold*
that slender foot
slap
a strap
with button
to shout
here is
my foot
here is
the shoe

    —Karren L. Alenier

A DOG.

A little monkey goes like a donkey that means to say that means to say that more sighs last goes. Leave with it. A little monkey goes like a donkey.

Jack and Jill remastered

A little pail is a pail is a pail.
Rings, a little,
Outside Mamaroneck High.
Four hands
Snap dandelion stalks.
Oh! This one blows.
Are we allowed?
Sure.
It blow blow blows.
Into the wa wa water.
Four feet
Go go go,
Frown, twists.
Dirt.
Their backs, on their backs
See stars—the universe, really.
The pail rings
Sleep now and oh the threat
Of mosquitos and midnight whispers.
Falls, snaps.
Snap.
Snap.
Snap.
Snap.
Snap.
Dreams of water too, are blue
And dreams were in this way
Dandelion water.
There where the dandelion
Can grow grow grow
Four legs make one dream baby
And dream baby dream.

—*Julien Berman*

A WHITE HUNTER.

A white hunter is nearly crazy.

flywheel in America: a father educates his children

I.
perhaps the title mister
missed the mark more
he was governor head
of state at least master
of a colony filled with
children the offspring
of his influence not just
the product of errant
sperm lodged in the life
raft of matrimonial eggs
his children offspring
of his desires the
shapeable minds subject
to his control yes governor
flywheel heavy but full of
kinetic energy streaming
ideas about what these little
people should know governor
requiring governess a private
instructor to mete his instruction

II.
the first governess met
his master list—music
German French a bit mousy but
smart except she returned to Europe
all too soon his children barely pro-
nouncing the "ik" versus "ique"
in the lingual variations of
music how angry how red-
faced mad his progeny made
him for their lacks better
double-dose the castor oil

III.
blond the second
governess a big strong
but stupid one—daughter
of a dairy farmer he said
to his kids read books and go
to American public school she knows
how to swim and exercise with you
here's a hoe she'll show you how
to plant even when she married
a baker the patriarch shaped his
day to see her to eat her
husband's cake

IV.
third and last governess
could drill German French
the practice of a musical
instrument she listened
obeyed the man of the house
the children still in public
school and free to run
the countryside found her
temper useless resented
the way their mother
his spouse owned this
American educated girl
ordered her personal
seamstress to design
a dress for the dear
governess doubled
her wage to dissuade
giving her hand too quick
to another rich man

V.
so a rich man with European flair
takes his children and wife
to a rural life where he can
govern strifeless dispense
the castor oil of his beliefs
one two three until he
achieves regularity
of a masculine machine
enforced by female spleen
how smart his children seem

—*Karren L. Alenier*

A LEAVE.

In the middle of a tiny spot and nearly bare there is a nice thing to say that wrist is leading. Wrist is leading.

after "A Leave"

I.
It is difficult to find
the middle. it is
nil
willing a wisp.

II.
A flame wallows in wax gladly.
Put your finger on it,
it's gone.
Then it jumps up again.

—*Rae Armantrout*

SUPPOSE AN EYES.

Suppose it is within a gate which open is open at the hour of closing summer that is to say it is so.

All the seats are needing blackening. A white dress is in sign. A soldier a real soldier has a worn lace a worn lace of different sizes that is to say if he can read, if he can read he is a size to show shutting up twenty-four.

Go red go red, laugh white.

Suppose a collapse in rubbed purr, in rubbed purr get.

Little sales ladies little sales ladies little saddles of mutton.

Little sales of leather and such beautiful beautiful, beautiful beautiful.

suppose

    (Afghanistan, August 2021)

Suppose it was us within that panicked throng outside the gate.

Suppose mouths open clamoring for mercy at the hour of closing.

Suppose the airport closing down the summer.

Suppose the summer closing down, seats on the aircraft collapsing.

Say which women are closing down.

Say which women wear blackening as a sign.

Which women's white dresses? Which hijabs of worn lace?

Which women's white lace blackened among soldiers outside the closing gates?

Suppose the different sizes of the crowd, suppose a collapse, rubbed pure.

Say which soldiers read the signs, the different sizes of signs.

Which signs shutting down the airport.

Suppose women in white dresses read the signs, their black head coverings.

Say which soldiers read the signs, which ones cannot read the signs.

Which generals or presidents ever read the signs.

Say which sales have saddled us.

Which leather saddles are so beautiful they must be blackened.

Suppose the flags red green blackening the whole show closing down,

Suppose women outside the gates at the hour of shutting down.

Suppose the collapse of a country.

    —Carolyne Wright

A SHAWL

A shawl is a hat and hurt and a red balloon and an under coat and a sizer a sizer of talk.

A shawl is a wedding, a piece of wax a little build. A shawl.

Pick a ticket, pick it in strange steps and with hollows. There is hollow hollow belt, a belt is a shawl.

A plate that has a little bobble, all of them, any so.

Please a round it is ticket.

It was a mistake to state that a laugh and a lip and a laid climb and a depot and a cultivator and little choosing is a point it.

a caul is not a shawl

Not the be nor end awl. A shrug for the shoulder when fall turns horizontal. Soft to touch if born from silky underbellies of fleece sheep shed before summer. So fine, pull it through a finger ring. So fine, fit for bride or traveler. Or king. Everything is reversable, two-faced, sure as faith. Which came first—tallit or cashmere? A sky-blue tail points to perfection. Not perfection, but display on the counter of piety. An industry can start up with less.

—*Barbara Goldberg*

BOOK.

Book was there, it was there. Book was there. Stop it, stop it, it was a cleaner, a wet cleaner and it was not where it was wet, it was not high, it was directly placed back, not back again, back, it was returned, it was needless, it put a bank, a bank when, a bank care.

Suppose a man a realistic expression of resolute reliability suggests pleasing itself white all white and no head does that mean soap. It does not so. It means kind wavers and little chance to beside beside rest. A plain.

Suppose ear rings, that is one way to breed, breed that. Oh chance to say, oh nice old pole. Next best and nearest a pillar. Chest not valuable, be papered.

Cover up cover up the two with a little piece of string and hope rose and green, green.

Please a plate, put a match to the seam and really then really then, really then it is a remark that joins many many lead games. It is a sister and sister and a flower and a flower and a dog and a colored sky a sky colored grey and nearly that nearly that let.

no book.

Only a few humans. Living in northern Canada. No books. A few humans. No banks either. No banks left. The run on banks dried the banks up.

No green. No green. Conflagration in the west, then the east. Flood first, then fires. Some black, same black, the ocean used to be so vast and blue. The dry unreliable raised land, the dust,

the dry cracked wheat buckling, this individual aridity. The raw end of futility, the futile rawness of the end. How can we survive.

Everyone is infected, infecting others, everyone is exposed, boneward, exposed, inside and out—there is no stopping it.

Until I get some confirmation, I refuse to go on and on, writing down these solitary words on this solitary page in this solitary room without flowers.

Until I get some confirmation, I refuse to go on with this solitary confinement, inventing the improbable, this improbable solitary confinement without dogs.

In which I am never alone, in which there is always noise, small crackling sounds, eerie sounds, creatures but not dogs, poking elongated noses out of bags.

Inside my closet, and I always try to keep the door shut—small mountain of intensity, and no one will ever acknowledge it. They always look as if nothing is there, while I point to it.

—Margo Taft Stever

PEELED PENCIL, CHOKE.

Rub her coke.

from the belly: a dialectic

I can lean upon a pencil.

a pencil is my
crutch do you get the
point the sharpness dulls
with every thrust
              I prefer
a slender
nib dipped
intensely
in what is
dark
in what is
indelible
      the American lead
so soft hardly immortality
the pencil real
popular number two
fill in the box to count
I do we do
        your vote
my preference a *bateau*
en flamme floating on the Seine
mon mari et moi hungry—his hair
afire by candlelight at midnight
in moonlight don't drink
the ink rather
let it let
it flow
so

—Karren L. Alenier

IT WAS BLACK, BLACK TOOK.

Black ink best wheel bale brown.

Excel lent not a hull house, not a pea soup, no bill no care, no precise no past pearl pearl goat.

blackened was

Blackened was it past or future now.
Whose care isn't it. Whose pearl.
Penned ultimate day.
Whose hello will the day house.

Whose care isn't it. Whose pearl.
What shell we make of today.
Whose hello will the day house.
Nothing comes of this climate.

What shell we make of today.
Hulled pearls or boll's husk.
Nothing comes of this climate.
Sea's surface sees oily clouds.

Hulled pearls or boll's husk.
A goat goes on and gone.
Sea's surface sees oily clouds.
How shell and wheel it reel.

A goat goes on and gone.
Hope banned herein turn.
How shell and wheel it reel.
What years in rhyme forget.

Hope banned herein turn.
No pea soup, no bill no care.
What years in rhyme forget.
My sallow eye sails a spark.

No pea soup, no bill no care.
Penned ultimate day.
My sallow eye sails a spark.
Blackened past future now.

—*Brad Richard*

THIS IS THIS DRESS, AIDER.

Aider, why, aider why whow, whow stop touch, aider whow, aider stop the muncher, muncher munchers.

A jack in kill her, a jack in, makes a meadowed king, makes a to let.

having words: a round

some history of some quarreling
    —The Making of Americans

quarreling is a form
of loving not
sparring a sport
quarreling is a branch
of ambition the
words heated to
a boil popping
one in the face
quarreling a row
of discord ear-
ache a pounding
of the heart in flam-
mable condition
ignited by shouting
match hot to
tender touch
arrow for the cross-
bow sporting a square
head glazier's
diamond cutting
what is glass
fitting for the
window time
we have defined
by the aim the goal
the need about
winning about
engaging about
quarreling

    quarreling is a form
    of loving not
    sparring a sport
    quarreling is a branch
    of ambition the
    words heated to
    a boil popping
    one in the face
    quarreling a row
    of discord ear-
    ache a pounding
    of the heart in flam-
    mable condition
    ignited by shouting
    match hot to
    tender touch
    arrow for the cross-
    bow sporting a square
    head glazier's
    diamond cutting
    what is glass
    fitting for the
    window time
    we have defined
    by the aim the goal
    the need about
    winning about
    engaging about
    quarreling

        quarreling is a form
        of loving not
        sparring a sport
        quarreling is a branch
        of ambition the
        words heated to
        a boil popping
        one in the face
        quarreling a row
        of discord ear-
        ache a pounding
        of the heart in flam-
        mable condition
        ignited by shouting
        match hot to
        tender touch
        arrow for the cross-
        bow sporting a square
        head glazier's
        diamond cutting
        what is glass
        fitting for the
        window time
        we have defined
        by the aim the goal
        the need about
        winning about
        engaging about
        quarreling

Reader 1 reads column one *solo voce*.
Reader 2 repeats column one with Reader 3 beginning column two after Reader 2 finishes line 3.
Reader 1 begins reading column three after Reader 3 finishes "sparring a sport."

    —*Karren L. Alenier*

APPENDIX A

How does one read *Tender Buttons*?

Approach each subpoem as if it were an abstract painting and allow yourself room to appreciate what thoughts come to you. Feel free to free associate.

This allows anyone, no matter their experience with reading texts by Stein, to pick up *Tender Buttons* without the fear of needing literary credentials.

Stein often implants suggestions for how to read her texts within the text of *Tender Buttons*.

For example, in "A carafe, that is a blind glass.", the first subpoem, Stein directs the reader to "an arrangement in a system to pointing." This is the author telling her audience that she will be making suggestions (system to pointing) in this arrangement of words. Moreover, while it isn't ordinary or familiar, it has order, and this difference will be proliferating. See?

> A CARAFE, THAT IS A BLIND GLASS.
>
> A kind in glass and a cousin, a spectacle and nothing strange a single hurt color and an arrangement in a system to pointing. All this and not ordinary, not unordered in not resembling. The difference is spreading.

Key words in a subpoem merit a search for the possible meanings and origins of the word in a dictionary. Often the best dictionary for looking up word origination is the *Oxford English Dictionary*, which includes an expanded history of each word. Key words thread through *Tender Buttons*, and if Stein uses a word more than once within a subpoem, that is a sign that she is up to something and the reader must dig in deeper.

Stein said that once you name something, you have used up that noun and so the word is dead. On the other hand, verbs and adverbs create activity.

While Stein presents as simply as possible, often using plain monosyllabic words, she operates within a system that usually harkens back to what she learned from her Harvard professor William James. Therefore she is pragmatic. Therefore there is always some logic behind what she is offering. This could be meaning or it could be method. Strings of words that don't make grammatical sense may be associated with some kind of process that might involve, for example, game-playing, musicality, or grammatical shakeup.

Stein's process could be even more complicated if one assumes she is attempting to create a sacred text. In reading Jewish sacred texts, Talmudic scholars use a set of reading techniques and clues about what is important in approaching difficult work as follows:

—repetition (things told twice)
—missing information (very common in sacred texts)
—key words repeated 3, 7, or 10 times in one passage or story
—seemingly unnecessary information
—repeating comparisons and contrasts with small differences
—difficult words and grammar
—ambiguity
—contradiction
—metaphor
—echoes from story to story
—issues of moral behavior
—juxtaposition
—symmetry (words or verses in a symmetrical pattern)
—out-of-order sequencing

And to this list, add masquerade and anagrams. Humor is also part of Stein's ludic (playful) landscape, and often manifests in odd word play.

Now, let's look at this nursery rhyme-ish subpoem of "Objects":

A DOG.

A little monkey goes like a donkey that means to say that means to say that more sighs last goes. Leave with it. A little monkey goes like a donkey.

Anagrammatically, the title could be G-O-A-D, an implement for riding a stubborn animal like a donkey. The text could be read as a sexual game with a little French inflection: my key (mon clé—rhymes with say) works like (goes like) your key (ton clé—t and d are close in sound) that means touché (means to say) and sigh (because anatomically we are alike—both females) but heck lead with it (leave with it—the goad perhaps?) because my key [still] works with your key.

Expect the unexpected and allow for contradiction. Stein was a polymath and *Tender Buttons* reaches into science, physics, psychology, religion, superstition, nursery rhymes, classic literature (especially the plays of William Shakespeare), American literature, philosophy (including logic), and more. Mathematics and geometry play into Stein's system of pointing. It's part of her logic and eye on cubism (think fractals).

Knowing Gertrude Stein's and Alice Toklas's biographies and the historical context of their time will also help illuminate *Tender Buttons*. This knowledge might help a reader buy into the premise that *Tender Buttons* is Stein's love poem to her wife Alice Toklas as well as the covenant as to how they will live with each other and what they will leave as their legacy.

Some of the subpoems of "Objects" are so short, a reader without biographical knowledge and historical context will have limited resources to draw on. Take for example:

A PETTICOAT.

A light white, a disgrace, an ink spot, a rosy charm.

A biographical and historical reading of these thirteen words might be that Stein was a rebel when it came to the clothes she chose to wear once she decided to be a writer in Paris. The Gibson Girl look (and there is a teenage photo of Stein dressed this way) required restrictive corsets and multiple petticoats under long dresses.

Such Victorian clothing made women uncomfortable to the degree that it pinched circulation and digestion, often making woman faint, and this clothing restricted movement and prevented the riding of bicycles. In 1896, Susan B. Anthony said the bicycle "has done more to emancipate women than anything else in the world." In the 1840s, suffragists like Amelia Bloomer and Elizabeth Cady Stanton made a point of helping women achieve more practical clothing like the bifurcated skirt and bloomers, but it was a battle long fought. Stein herself never wore pants or rode a bicycle, but she carefully thought out what would make her comfortable, choosing (once Alice was part of her life) a long roomy skirt, blouse, and vest. Both she and Alice discarded the Victorian corset and petticoats.

Biographical readings might also include her long relationship with Pablo Picasso, cubism, and various visual artists in whose work Gertrude and Leo Stein invested. Stein treated all aspects of her life equally in *Tender Buttons*, and often these elements arise simultaneously, showing Stein's dazzling dimensionality, where one word, phrase, or sentence projects many associations at the same time.

For detailed discussions of *Tender Buttons* "Objects" (section I), search Karren Alenier's publishing blog at https://alenier.blogspot.com.

APPENDIX B

Ways for invoking the Steinian muse (listed without prejudice to which comes first):

1. Biography.
Stein, her family, and friends had compelling biographies that might marry up to a segment of *Tender Buttons*.

2. Other works by Gertrude Stein.
Stein had a habit of pointing to other works she had written. Also there seemed to be no boundaries between genres for Stein and therefore one can consider everything she wrote (novels, plays, libretti) as poetry.

3. Words and their roots.
Just when you are ready to throw up your hands and say you cannot be inspired by Stein's tender buttons, especially the fragments containing only a few words, this is when you should go to the dictionary with a word and look up its root meaning. Often there is a universe in the most unassuming word that cracks open a path.

4. Grammatical and linguistic constructs.
Stein was intent on revitalizing the English language. For the most part, she chose Anglo-Saxon words, often of one syllable. Sometimes her repetitions show slight variations as if she were conjugating that word (changing its form based on the sentence structure).

5. Making words sing.
Just as the reader should step back from a tender button as if it were an abstract painting, Stein's audience should read the work out loud to hear its music. Then one should free associate. Stein expected her readers to engage with her work and not be passive.

These tips on reading Stein are based on years of leading online discussions in the Coursera MOOC Modern and Contemporary Poetry (ModPo). —KLA

CONTRIBUTORS

Karren LaLonde Alenier was the first poet published (1975) by The Word Works. Karren is author of eight poetry collections, including *Looking for Divine Transportation*, winner of the 2002 Towson University Prize for Literature, *The Anima of Paul Bowles*, 2016 top staff pick at the Grolier Bookshop (Boston), and her most recent book *how we hold on* from Broadstone Books, 2021. *Gertrude Stein Invents a Jump Early On*, her jazz opera with composer Bill Banfield, premiered June 2005 in New York by Encompass New Opera Theatre. https://www.alenier.com

Indran Amirthanayagam in 2020 published three poetry books: *The Migrant States* (Hanging Loose Press, New York) *Sur l'île nostalgique* (L'Harmattan, Paris) and *Lírica a tiempo* (Mesa Redonda, Lima). Author of 20 books and winner of the Paterson Prize, writing in English, Spanish, French, Portuguese, and Haitian Creole, he edits *The Beltway Poetry Quarterly*.

Rae Armantrout is author of sixteen books of poems, including *Finalists* (2022); *Conjure* (2020); *Wobble* (2018), finalist for the National Book Award; and *Versed* (2009), winner the Pulitzer Prize and the National Book Critics Circle Award in 2010. In 2021, she was judge of the Yale Younger Poet award.

Mary Armour, a long-standing participant in Modern and Contemporary American Poetry (ModPo) forums, has loved the work of Gertrude Stein for years. She was born and grew up in Zimbabwe and now works in southern Africa as a writer and editor with human-rights organizations.

Carrie Bennett is author of three poetry books: *Lost Letters and Other Animals*, *The Land Is a Painted Thing*, and *biography of water*. In 2004, she won The Word Works Washington Prize. She holds an MFA in poetry from the Iowa Writers' Workshop and currently teaches writing at Boston University.

Margo Berdeshevsky, NYC born, writes from Paris. Her last collection: *Before the Drought* (Glass Lyre Press/ National Poetry Series finalist). Newest collections: *It Is Still Beautiful to Hear the Heart Beat* from Salmon Poetry, and *Kneel Said the Night* (a hybrid book in half notes) from Sundress Publications. http://margoberdeshevsky.com

Julien Berman is a freshman at Harvard University. His stories and poems have appeared in *34th Parallel*, *The Raven Review*, and *Indolent Books*. In 2019, he won The Word Works Jacklyn Potter Young Poets Competition. He has also won national Scholastic Art and Writing Awards.

Andrea Carter Brown's most recent poetry collection is *September 12*, which was awarded the 2022 IPPY Silver Medal in Poetry. Author of *Domestic Karma*, *The Disheveled Bed*, and *Brook & Rainbow*. She lives in Los Angeles, serving as Series Editor of The Word Works Washington Prize. https://www.andreacarterbrown.com

Susana H. Case is the award-winning author of eight books of poetry, most recently *The Damage Done* (Broadstone Books, 2022), and co-editor with Margo Taft Stever of *I Wanna Be Loved by You: Poems on Marilyn Monroe* (Milk & Cake Press, 2022). https://www.susanahcase.com

Grace Cavalieri is Maryland's tenth Poet Laureate. She founded and still produces "The Poet and the Poem" for public radio, and podcasts, now from The Library of Congress, celebrating its 45th year in 2022. Author of numerous books and produced plays, her latest is *The Long Game: Poems Selected & New* (The Word Works, 2022).

Nikia Chaney is author of *to stir &* (The Word Works 2022), *us mouth* (University of Hell Press, 2018), and two chapbooks, *Sis Fuss* (Orange Monkey Publishing, 2012) and *ladies, please* (Dancing Girl Press, 2012). She served as Inlandia Literary Laureate 2016-2018. Her poetry has been published in *Sugarhouse Review*, *491*, *Iowa Review*, and others.

Roberto Christiano's poems have appeared in *Prairie Schooner* (Pushcart nominated), *Beltway Quarterly*, *Silk Road*, *Sow's Ear Poetry Review*, *New Verse News*, and *The Washington Post*. His latest book is *Port of Leaving* (Expanded Edition), published by Finishing Line Press. His poetry has been anthologized in *The Gávea-Brown Book of Portuguese-American Poetry*. https://robertochristiano.weebly.com

Henry Crawford is author of two collections of poetry, *American Software* (CW Books, 2017) and *Binary Planet* (The Word Works, 2020). He won first prize in the 2019 World Food Poetry Competition. http://www.henrycrawfordpoetry.com

Michael Davis: poet, journalist, tanguero, classical guitarist. His book *Prodigal* was published by New Academia Press in 2019. Mica Press published his chapbook *Upon Waking* in 1997. His work has appeared in *Poet Lore*, *Hika*, *Gargoyle*, and a number of anthologies, including *Open Door*, *Winners*, and *Written in Arlington*.

Denise Duhamel's most recent book of poetry is *Second Story* (Pittsburgh, 2021). Her other titles include *Scald*, *Blowout*, *Ka-Ching!*, *Two and Two*, *Queen for a Day: Selected and New Poems*, *The Star-Spangled Banner*, and *Kinky*. She teaches in the MFA program at Florida International University in Miami.

Amy Feinstein is the author of *Gertrude Stein and the Making of Jewish Modernism*. She teaches ninth grade English at a public high school in the Bronx.

Barbara Goldberg has authored eight prize-winning poetry books, including *Breaking & Entering: New and Selected Poems*. Recipient of fellowships from the National Endowment for the Arts, she translated and edited contemporary Israel poetry. Goldberg, Series Editor of Word Works International Editions, has selected poets translated from Kurdish, Croatian, and Ancient Greek for publication.

Harold M. Greenwald is a computer scientist and musician living in Bethesda, Maryland. As a poetry enthusiast, he participates in the University of Pennsylvania's Modern & Contemporary American Poetry ("ModPo") series in addition to several poetry reading and discussion groups. He has recently been studying the work of Gertrude Stein.

Donald Illich has published poetry in *Iowa Review*, *LIT*, *Passages North*, *Nimrod*, *Fourteen Hills*, and other publications. He is the author of *Chance Bodies* (The Word Works, 2018).

Jacqueline Johnson, is a multi-disciplined artist in writing and fiber arts. She is the author of *A Woman's Season* from Main Street Rag Press and *A Gathering of Mother Tongues*, winner of the Third Annual White Pine Press Poetry Award.

Hiram Larew's poems have appeared in *Contemporary American Voices*, *Poetry South*, *Best Poetry Online*, and *Amsterdam Quarterly*. His fifth collection, *Mud Ajar*, was issued in 2021 by Atmosphere Press. https://www.hiramlarewpoetry.com

JoAnne McFarland is an artist, poet, curator, and Artistic Director of Artpoetica Project Space in Brooklyn, NY. She has artwork in the permanent collections of Library of Congress and Columbus Museum of Art, among others. Her innovative digital poetry collections include *Pullman* and *Tracks of My Tears*. Collections include *Identifying the Body*, *Stills*, *Acid Rain*, and *Loose Horse in the Valley*. https://www.joannemcfarland.com

Kevin McLellan is author of: *Ornitheology* (The Word Works, 2018), *Tributary* (Barrow Street, 2015), *Hemispheres* (Fact-Simile Editions, 2019), *[box]* (Letter [r] Press, 2016), and *Round Trip* (Seven Kitchens, 2010). His video production company, Duck Hunting with the Grammarian, produced *Dick* (Berlin Short Film Festival, Flickers' Rhode Island Film Festival, and others). https://kevmclellan.com

Nils Michals of Santa Cruz, CA, is author of four poetry collections, including *Lure* (Pleiades, 2004), *Come Down to Earth* (Bauhan, 2014), *Room* (Sting & Honey, 2020), and *Gembox* (winner, The Word Works Washington Prize, 2018). His work has appeared in *Tupelo Quarterly*, *[PANK]*, and *Posit*. He teaches at West Valley College. http://www.nilsmichals.com

Brad Richard is author of, among other books, *Parasite Kingdom* (The Word Works, 2019, winner of the 2018 Tenth Gate Prize). His most recent chapbook is *In Place* (Seven Kitchens Press, 2021, selected for the Robin Becker Series). He lives in New Orleans. https://bradrichard.org

Margery M. Ross, electronic legal research pioneer, was an Account Manager for LexisNexis databases. Following retirement, she joined the online class Modern and Contemporary American Poetry (ModPo) and a weekly in-person group in Washington, DC, that discusses poetry. Her poem "Last Bus" was published by *The New Verse News* in 2020.

Martha Sanchez-Lowery's poetry appears in *Gargoyle*, *Hispanic Culture Review*, and the anthologies *Written in Arlington* and *Knocking on the Door of the White House*. Her poem "The Dark Earth Call" was set to dance by Jane Franklin Dance Company. She produced Poetry Alive at IOTA–10th and 20th Anniversary CDs.

Roger Sedarat is author of *Dear Regime: Letters to the Islamic Republic* (winner, Ohio UP's Hollis Summers Poetry Prize, 2007), *Ghazal Games* (Ohio UP, 2011), and *Haji as Puppet: an Orientalist Burlesque* (winner, The Word Works Tenth Gate Prize, 2017). He teaches in the MFA Program at Queens College.

Lisa Sewell is author of *The Way Out*, *Name Withheld*, *Long Corridor*, and *Impossible Object*, winner of The Word Works Tenth Gate Prize 2014. Her work has appeared in *Split Rock Review*, *Louisiana Review*, *Prairie Schooner*, and *Porter Gulch*. She lives in Philadelphia and teaches in the English Department at Villanova University. https://lisasewell.com

Margo Taft Stever's seven poetry collections include *The End of Horses* (Broadstone Books, 2022), *Cracked Piano* (CavanKerry Press, 2019) and *Ghost Moose* (Kattywompus Press, 2019). She is the founder of the Hudson Valley Writers Center and founding and current co-editor of Slapering Hol Press. https://margotaftstever.com

Miles Waggener is author of four books of poetry: *Phoenix Suites*, *Sky Harbor*, *Desert Center*, and most recently *Superstition Freeway*, published by The Word Works. A recipient of The Word Works Washington Prize, he also received individual grants from the Arizona Commission on the Arts and the Nebraska Arts Council.

Lillo Way's poetry collection, *Lend Me Your Wings*, was launched in 2021 by Shanti Arts Publishing. Her *Dubious Moon* won the Slapering Hol Chapbook Contest. She is winner of the E.E. Cummings Award and a *Florida Review* Editors' Prize. Her writing has appeared in *Poet Lore*, *New Letters*, and many anthologies. https://www.lilloway.com

Nancy White's poetry collections are *Sun, Moon, Salt* (winner of the Washington Prize), *Detour*, and *Ask Again Later*. Her work has appeared in *Black Warrior Review*, *FIELD*, *Ploughshares*, and many other journals. She serves as president and co-editor-in-chief at The Word Works and teaches at SUNY Adirondack.

Carolyne Wright's latest book is *Masquerade* (Lost Horse Press, 2021), a memoir in poetry. She teaches for Richard Hugo House in her native Seattle. A Pushcart Prize Contributing Editor with a 2022-2023 Fulbright Scholar Award to Bahia, Brazil, she has 17 earlier books and anthologies of poetry, essays, and translation.

Bill Yarrow, Professor of English at Joliet Junior College, is the author of six full-length books of poetry and six poetry chapbooks. His poems have been published in many journals, including *Poetry International*, *Confrontation*, *Gargoyle*, *FRiGG*, *[PANK]*, *Contrary*, *Diagram*, *Thrush*, *Rhino*, *Chiron Review*, *Magma*, and *Mantis*. https://billyarrow.godaddysites.com

Burgi Zenhaeusern (she/her) is the author of the chapbook *Behind Normalcy* (CityLit Press, 2020), winner of the Harriss Poetry Prize. She is a consulting editor for *River Mouth Review*. https://burgizenhaeusern.com

Jason Zuzga is the author of the poetry collection *Heat Wake*. He is the Other/Nonfiction Editor of *Fence* magazine. He has published poetry and nonfiction in *Seneca Review*, *The Paris Review*, *jubilat*, and elsewhere.

INDEX BY AUTHOR

Alenier, Karren L.: 15, 17, 19, 21, 23, 25, 27, 29, 31, 33, 39, 41, 45, 55, 65, 67, 97, 105, 111, 114, 125, 129
Amirthanayagam, Indran: 59
Armantrout, Rae: 117
Armour, Mary: 63
Bennett, Carrie: 79
Berdeshevsky, Margo: 107
Berman, Julien: 113
Brown, Andrea Carter: 71
Case, Susana H.: 109
Cavalieri, Grace: 77
Chaney, Nikia: 69
Christiano, Roberto: 81
Crawford, Henry: 47
Davis, Michael: 37
Duhamel, Denise: 53
Feinstein, Amy: 103
Goldberg, Barbara: 121
Greenwald, Harold M.: 43
Illich, Donald: 95
Johnson, Jacqueline: 61
Larew, Hiram: 57
McFarland, JoAnne: 83
McLellan, Kevin: 99
Michals, Nils: 49
Richard, Brad: 127
Ross, Margery M.: 93
Sanchez-Lowery, Martha: 101
Sedarat, Roger: 35
Sewell, Lisa: 89
Stever, Margo Taft: 123
Waggener, Miles: 85
Way, Lillo: 87
White, Nancy: 75
Wright, Carolyne: 119
Yarrow, Bill: 91
Zenhaeusern, Burgi: 51
Zuzga, Jason: 72

ABOUT THE WORD WORKS

Since its founding in 1974, The Word Works has steadily published volumes of contemporary poetry and presented public programs. Its imprints include The Washington Prize, The Tenth Gate Prize, The Hilary Tham Capital Collection, and International Editions.

Monthly, The Word Works offers free programs in its Café Muse Literary Salon. Starting in 2023, the winners of the Jacklyn Potter Young Poets Competition will be presented in the June Café Muse program.

As a 501(c)3 organization, The Word Works has received awards from the National Endowment for the Arts, the National Endowment for the Humanities, the D.C. Commission on the Arts & Humanities, the Witter Bynner Foundation, Poets & Writers, The Writer's Center, Bell Atlantic, the David G. Taft Foundation, and others, including many generous private patrons.

An archive of artistic and administrative materials in the Washington Writing Archive is housed in the George Washington University Gelman Library. The Word Works is a member of the Community of Literary Magazines and Presses and its books are distributed by Small Press Distribution.

wordworksbooks.org